DOWN IN THE VALLEY

"WEEPING MAY ENDURE FOR A NIGHT"

Dr. Dorothy J. Thomas

William & Harriet

8/2/16

Christ is the God we
serve. Be blessed
in all that you do for
His Glory!

Praise for
Down in the Valley

*H*aving an ongoing relationship with God is the only
way that I was able to endure the long and
painful journey of grief due to the loss of
my mom. I lamented to God repeatedly
for help, as Dorothy did in this incredible
book. We were both *Down in the Valley*,
but God sustained the both of us, as only
He can.

Dorothy and I met at a Christian con-
ference where she was a participant and

I was the presenter. Her knowledge and professionalism intrigued me by the way she answered a question that I had posed. After I finished my presentation, we chatted a while longer. From that short conversation, I could tell that she was a very caring and spiritual woman of God. It wasn't until months later that I found out she was actually *Dr.* Dorothy Thomas, the Christian counselor. Because of her humbleness, she never revealed her status to me. That was five years ago and we've been very dear and true friends ever since.

Dorothy definitely has a way with words, which is clearly evident in the following pages of this, her second book. Some authors have a hard time finding their own writing style and voice — not Dorothy. Her literary writing style and unique voice are truly a treasure.

I was really encouraged and comforted by reading *Down in the Valley*. Never before have I read such a rich and poignant story of true love that lasted, as the wedding vows say, "Until death do us part." While reading this book, I had to stop several times because the fluency and depth of the content touched something deep within me. The sweet purity of love is definitely captured in these pages. The agony and pain is also clearly defined. While reading, I could literally hear Andrew Rieu's instrumental version of *Love Theme*.

Down in the Valley blends poetic prose with literary distinctness, which showcases Dorothy's versatile writing style. She manages to join together her triumphant love story, painful experience with grief, and her love relationship with God, while selflessly reaching out to assist others who are going through the same healing process.

Yvonne Randle

Author of The *Secret of Creating Loving Relationships.*

Table of Contents

Seasons

Dedication

To my beloved husband, Roosevelt
Thomas, who was the love of my life.

"Sail On"

Beloved,
The waters of life are not easily crossed.
Yet we sailed away on a voyage
Searching for continuous adventure you and
I sailed away, finding sandy
Beaches of hope, distant lands of joy,
filled with life's unknown treasures.
You and I landed on the shores
of wonder, exploring the beauty
of love, family and faith.
You and I faced the darkness of the deep, yet
received the light of victory.
You and I persevered through
the storms of the raging sea,
With waves that seemed relentless,
yet we were given peace and an
Everlasting calm.   You and I made the
journey and "You" have moved on
To the other side of the sea.
'Sail On' the mast is high, Sail On;
the winds are strong,
Sail On − The shore is at hand.

Acknowledgements

*A*ll the honor, glory, and praise belong to God who orders my steps and is the head of my life.

To my family and friends who helped me through this valley experience, thank you for your love, support, and many prayers.

To those who have experienced the loss of a spouse, it is my prayer that you received the comfort you needed.   Be encouraged and know that the God of Abraham, Isaac, and Jacob, still lives and

reigns over our lives today. May He bless
you with His grace and mercy, and restore
you to a place of peace.

REFLECTIONS
LOVE BORN, LOVE LIVED, LOVE LOST

CHAPTER ONE

"WEEPING MAY ENDURE FOR A NIGHT"

*I*t was a cold winter day, the clouds were gray and the wind was howling. I sat near the window thinking of us, and memories of days gone by. Thinking of our lives together with all the joys, disappointments, and funny times with our children. Thinking of the love we shared and the special events that occurred during our life together. I was shaking as I thought back over our lives and the tears of sadness and joy were mixed together, confusing and yet a small amount of clarity was present.

Life was not a bowl of cherries, but more like a glass of wine, rich in color, with a light fragrance with the appearance of comfort.   Our life together would flow endlessly with memories that seemed to go on forever.   "Happy days are here again." A frequent tune we would sing after one of life's storms. You know the kind of storm that takes you to a place of uncertainty.   You can't figure out how the holes in the checkbook will be plugged up, or how all the bills will be paid. Somehow, God brought us through many more storms. When the storm had passed over, we would sing this song and rejoice.

I recalled a time when I became very ill, not sure at the time if I would live a full and vibrant life again. A constant barrage of questions flooded our minds and hearts. We talked about my ability to care for the children, among other things. My heart was heavy and I admit I was very frightened during this storm. One day, Honey sat by my bed and read the 23rd Psalm to me. He reminded me of my faith and the belief he had in God and our love. He was gentle and tender, soft-spoken and reassuring as his words pierced my heart. "Everything will be all right," he said, and it was. I made a full recovery and we would sing this song again. He was a strong man of faith and love. This was one of my most memorable moments. What an awesome God we serve.

My thoughts continued to be flooded with so many beautiful memories over the years. Raising our boys was both challenging and delightful. My husband loved sports, football, baseball, and basketball. He made sure his sons would follow in his footsteps by teaching them the "game," as he would say, and they learned and played well. He coached, mentored, sponsored and cheered them in every effort they made. Of course, I did my share of the cheering as well, and to this day, I am still an avid fan of these sports.

Well, sports was not our only challenge. The boys were involved in Scouting and Honey served as den leader. He helped them make cars, fold the American flag and taught them discipline, and respect for self and others. He was honored for teaching the den how to fold the flag and presented it at a Pack Night ceremony. This, he said, was one of the proudest moments he had experienced as a father and mentor, not only to his son, but to other boys. We began to sing his song, "Happy Days Are Here Again." Indeed, this was a very happy time in our life.

We also encountered times of disappointment and sadness. My husband always believed in the sanctity of family, which of course, included parents. It was

21

very important to him, "a necessity for growth and stability," he would say. His family would receive a terrible blow one late fall evening. He would be called to the hospital and told that his father was dying. He remained at this father's side until death. This would, of course, cause him emotional pain and grief. But he would constantly talk about the need to reflect on happy time. He felt that happy memories and family would help carry us through the trying time. For me, memories can be very rewarding, but they can also be very painful, taking you into a valley, but faith will get you through.

We shared many years together, though now they seemed to be nearing a close. The doctor said his condition was critical, and didn't know if he would survive his illness. He suffered for many years with diabetes and was being challenged with the complications of this disease.

Yes, we knew what the doctor said, but we were Christians, you see, and our hope was in Jesus. We continued to hold on to our faith, which gave us strength in spite of our uncertainty. I must admit, I thought that I wouldn't survive, either.

The Man Behind the Illness

He was a man of faith, praying for God's divine healing, as well as the courage to accept His will.

"Honey, was a "tall glass of water," refreshing and very filling. I admired and respected Honey's strength, courage, and devotion to his family. These qualities caused me to nickname him "Honey," sweet and long-lasting!

He was about 6′ 1″, of medium build, with caramel-brown skin. He was just as handsome as could be, and had flair of distinction. This tender and very compassionate man of courage and strength was sweet, solid, yet flexible. He was a man of substance and integrity, never compromising his principles, but open to the voice of truth. His love was honest and sincere, with a depth that could reach the bottom of the sea. There was a certain authority about him that seemed to permeate any room he walked into.

Honey was very excited about the possibilities of a future, especially since he had wondered if he would ever have one. He was young and immature when he was drafted into the army. He was apprehensive about going to war, going to an unknown land. His apprehensions, however, never interfered with his sense of duty.

He was a soldier who had a story to tell, and well, there were times when he would disclose the hidden pain of war. Honey talked often about times spent in Vietnam, and the mysteries that surrounded a people in their search for hope. I wondered often about the mysteries that shrouded him at times, like a haze of forgetfulness that refused to go into the abyss. He learned the meaning of war and all of it horrors.

Freedom, he would often say, "it's not, and never will be, free."

Honey was very disciplined and believed in order. Bed sheets tucked tight at each end, he often flipped a coin to show me his technique. Of course, I would chuckle at his exhibition of male prowess, but realized he gained strength from his orderly mannerisms.

The separation from family, friends, and "the theft" as he would call it, of his youth weighed heavily on him.

Honey fought many battles, not just the ones on the battlefield in a foreign land, but rather, the battlefield of life with its many disappointments. One was a career that would never come to fruition; one of the many spoils of war. He felt he had been robbed of his dreams. It was his dream to teach high school and coach one of his favorite sports. However, going back to college was no longer a heartfelt desire for him. The war left him feeling alone, sometimes preferring to be a loner. His subtle fear of having friends too close would haunt him due to the loss of his army buddies during combat. However, he never allowed this to stop him from being all that God wanted him to be. He would often remark about the goodness of God's love and mercy. Honey's gratitude to God for returning him home after serving in Vietnam was echoed by his words of praise and thanksgiving. A good man, oh yes, he was one to be remembered.

Despite Honey's illness, he seemed calm while being confronted with a calamity of this magnitude. He fought what the Bible calls "a good fight."

~~~~~~~~~~~~~~~~~~~~~~~~~~~~~~~~~~~~

At the Hospital

During the time we shared in Honey's hospital room, we talked a lot about our boys; how proud we were of them and the women they had chosen to share their lives with. The joy of our grandchildren, their funny smiles, each having their own personalities. He thought this was especially hilarious, the way they expressed themselves. Our reflections would last for hours, mostly with me talking, and of course, he would listen attentively.

His love for me saturated all available spaces in his hospital room, and I returned his affection with the same intensity. We were a pair, you see, always together, even in the presence of others; it was always… just us.

From My Hospital Memories:

Our sons are here with us now, and Honey is awake, looking at them with hope and pride, yet I can see the pain in his eyes. He doesn't want them to see how sick he is, but of course they know, we all know — he's in critical condition. Our sons know this will be a difficult journey, however, they allow their dad to maintain his dignity by not letting him see the deep concern that is tucked away in their hearts. They laugh and talk about sports or one of his favorite western movies. Their love is tender and childlike, overtly showing the most powerful emotion a son can share with his father. That emotion is love.

Honey continues to struggle now; the conclusion of his journey is drawing nigh. The family is here, in and out, taking turns to be with him, and me, well I am still looking out the window, at the gray sky and seeing the wind lift the leaves from the trees.

Turning my attention back to him, I notice he's fallen asleep.

Mournfully, I once again begin looking out the window at the cloudy gray sky and watching the wind lift the leaves from the trees. I begin to reflect back on our lives, and remember; oh – our memories.

Summer of 1967 – The Courtship

It was the summer of 1967 and I was wearing a white empire style dress with little yellow flowers at the midriff. My hair was long and, well, let's just say I was considered very attractive by some, but especially by him. Honey was wearing his army dress uniform, looking as if he'd just stepped out of a magazine. Handsome! Well, that was putting it mildly.

As the saying goes, it was love at first sight. Well, for me it was love at first glance, and he later admitted, it was the same for him. Many days we talked and visited with our families, and impatiently waited for our alone time.

This was a time when the South embraced a segregated mindset, and when affordable activities for young people were limited, especially the ones that afforded them alone time. He asked if he could see me later, and of course I replied, "Yes," and invited him to dinner. After dinner, we went for a walk, and later sat on the porch and continued to talk while having a glass of sweet tea; a Southern favorite, even today. For the next month, we spent what seemed like every waking moment together.

Our courtship was fun and adventurous. We spent months writing, talking on the phone, and seeing each other before he had to leave for his duty assignments in the states. There were, however, periods of separation, which were very difficult for both of us.

We pledged our love to each other and promised never to be separated once his tour of duty was over. We kept our promise.

~~~~~~~~~~~~~~~~

One Sunday evening, we vowed our love to each other in the chapel of the church. There were candles, flowers, family and friends, but most importantly, God was present. The minister blessed our union and we promised to always be there for each other.

~~~~~~~~~~~~~~~~

Now we find ourselves at the crossroad between life and death and yet, we are still here for each other.

CHAPTER TWO

*O*ur extended families had gone from the hospital. He was sleeping more now, yet when he was awake, he'd continue to stare at me. I continued to talk to him. I loved him so much. My heart pounded with each breath I took.

I sensed he knew I was afraid, but I had to refrain from any open expression of being frightened. He seemed very tired, nonetheless, somewhat peaceful. It was as if his body was weighed down with a huge boulder, and with each breath it got heavier, yet he knew it would all be over soon.

That night was uneventful; yet, the morning brought a new challenge. He seemed so very tired; exhausted, really. His breathing was different and his gaze upon me was strange. He appeared very distant, and at the same time, very close.

"Can you see me?" I asked.

He nodded in the affirmative.

"Are you tired?"

Again, he nodded. "Yes."

I didn't know what to feel. I was in a state of denial regarding the possible finality of our life together. I knew I had to remain calm and hopeful. "Very tired?" I asked again.

He nodded. "Yes."

"You can take a nap," I said.

He closed his eyes.

I briefly looked away, and when I turned back toward him, he was staring at me. "Beloved," I said. "Go on, you take a nap, I'm not going anywhere, I'll be right here." I was feeling so many things all at once: confusion, panic, sorrow, but I knew I had to show strength. Prayer and hope were the order of the day.

The Time Has Come

Sadly, we watched as he gradually slipped from this life to his new life with God. As we watched and listened to the sounds of death take its final grip, the reality of the moment was now here. Nothing can prepare you for the realism of finality. Despite the obvious, we were still bewildered and overwhelmed with sadness, shock, and hopelessness.

Thank God, his countenance appeared to be one of peace. No struggle — but victory! He was at rest now. His days of pain and suffering were over. The sadness and disappointments brought on by this life were finally behind him.

THE COLOR OF MOURNING

I wore black that day; the day my world stood still and I was unable to move. The tears burned the very wells of my eyes and flowed against a black and endless backdrop of sadness and despair. The sky was always gray and the clouds seemed to be dark, all the time. I could hear people crying, feel their touches and sense their sadness…but not really.

The church was filled with family and friends dressed in black. Before viewing his body, people stopped to embrace me and share their condolences. The atmosphere was very somber, sad, and quiet. I could hear an occasional sound of someone crying softly, as if not to disturb anyone else.

I remember turning towards our sons, and seeing the reflection of deep pain in their eyes. I remember that look of pain, from that day to this. In a daze, I wondered, "What is happening now? What is going on?" Then all of a sudden, reality hit, sharply, like a cold splash of water! Have you ever had the feeling that you wanted to be somewhere else and yet you couldn't? Well, that was what I was feeling, so I decided to escape by looking out the window. It was dark; the wind was still blowing and lifting the leaves from the trees.

As the funeral was taking place, I noticed a different feeling; that of physical pain in my chest. My body ached. The tears had left what seemed to be permanent white stains down my cheeks.

The cemetery was quiet. The weather was cold, with occasional sprinkles of rain. It appeared the weather was sad, just like me.

We said our final goodbyes, granting him the military honors he deserved. The flag waved, the soldiers saluted, and

I — could — not — move.   The minister spoke, the family cried, and I — could — not — move.   The soldier blew taps, the air felt colder, the rain was flowing, and still I could not move. I wondered why I was there. Why was this happening and why was my beloved husband gone? My body was frozen as if in a time warp, suspended in the air.   What was happening to me?

We began the procession back to the church for the repast.   This seemed to be a long ride back to a reality that I was not ready to face.   People began to refresh themselves with food and fellowship. There was some laughter and the atmosphere was pleasant, yet I was still not moving.

Oh! I was so confused, hurt, lonely, and devastated. But of course I was gracious and pleasant to the guests. I was thankful to God for His grace and mercy, even though I was still in more emotional pain than I ever could have imagined. They called it mourning. I called it foreign...alien...uncharted territory. My life was now on perpetual hold, suspended, in limbo. I hardly noticed people leaving.

I was in my own world. I walked to the window and looked out at the rain. The wind was still blowing, and yes, lifting the leaves from the trees.

CHAPTER THREE

REALITY

*R*eality had reared its ugly head. I must embrace life alone, a widow. How *I hated that word.*

First, I must digress by starting the journey and reflecting on our beginning.

Hard work was not foreign to us and we believed if we worked hard and stayed focused in our faith, we would be granted the desires of our hearts, as described in the Holy Scriptures. We looked forward to the adventures that lay ahead of us with enthusiasm and expectations.

Our love gave us a beautiful son. We viewed him with awe as he wiggled his little fingers and toes. Now we had responsibility, and could no longer be selfish with our love. Our son was a blessing and joy. Honey began to take his role, as father, very seriously, pampering and giving comfort, only as a father could. As our son grew older, we became involved in Little League, school programs, and such. What a joy we found in those times. I fondly remember.

Continuing to reflect on a time of joy and fulfillment...after many years, we were blessed again with another son, who was the apple of all of our eyes. He brought us joy and we felt young again. We'd begun another chapter in our lives, one with a teenager and a young son. What a balance that was.   Two sons, many years apart, well, let's just say, joy has its challenges.

Being a "dad," as Honey would say, was one of the most important jobs he could ever have.   He championed his sons in everything their hearts and minds would attempt to achieve.   He taught them baseball, basketball, football, and anything having to do with sports.   He was an athlete and shared that charac-teristic of himself with his sons.   He expressed the need to share everything he could with them that modeled self-dis-cipline, respect, teamwork, and spiritual growth. He demonstrated the life-style he wanted to pass on to our sons; parenting and a strong sense of family and home life. He would often say, *"Being a man requires the strength to love a woman, the ambition to raise a son, and leave a legacy."* I thought this was so profound, I wrote it in a card once, just a word of encouragement for him.

Honey was successful in leaving his sons a legacy, one that would value family and commitment as a husband. They are now husbands and fathers, following in the footsteps of their father and continuing the legacy with their sons.

Family was very important to us because we were raised with large families and strong family systems. Obedience, respect, compassion, and love for one another were not only expected, but was reciprocated. There was no such thing as abusing a child, but rather discipline with love, and acknowledgement of strengths and weakness. Needless to say, there were times when we needed to acknowledge the weak areas as well as highlight the strong ones. Our sons were able to accelerate in school with our support and guidance.

~~~~~~~~~~~~~~~~

As our children grew older, leaving home and going to college, this began another chapter in our lives. I began to explore a career in a different area, and

Honey began to explore his passion for fixing things. We also began to explore each other in a different and more mature way. We could laugh at the hard times once we were past them, however, there were times when we would cry together in the midst of those challenges. Our respect for each other began to be our strength. We became closer than before, so close that we didn't like to be anywhere else but with each other. We had our date nights, which we did not allow anyone to infringe upon. We shopped together, cooked together, and became content — just being together!

Wow, what a legacy we had!

~~~~~~~~~~~~~~~~

And then in a moment, part of my life was gone forever, with only reflections and memories left. The wind was still blowing, lifting the leaves from the trees.

I was alone now, not knowing what to do, feel, or think. This was horrible! I had loved a man for forty years and now I could only love a memory, a reflection, and a thought. I felt now as if I could break every dish in the kitchen. As if I could scream to the top of voice. When Honey became ill, my sister told me that during trying times, "When you can't seem to pray through the pain, ask God to comfort you and He will." I began calling, lamenting, crying to Him for comfort— He sustained me.

When a surgeon performs an operation, an incision must be made to the affected area. My affected area was the "affectionate sentiment" called the heart. The wound was opened, so there was no need for an incision. With each heartbeat, the intensity of the pain took my breath away. Nights were met with screaming and agony, which exacerbated the wound, causing fear to abound. "Oooohh! Help me," I would cry, daily.

And now, through it all, I once again began to pray and ask God to comfort me, and He heard my prayer and gave me comfort.

The Color of Mourning is Gray

When we mourn, our hearts try to escape the reality of loss. We encounter emotional pain that is beyond the stretch of the imagination.

Remember, gray is merely a temporary color, lasting for one moment in time. Be encouraged, you are just having a gray day.

We are more aware of the process of grieving a death, rather than the process of dying.

Bereavement is a state of loss, grief is the emotional response to loss and mourning consists of culturally prescribed ways of displaying one's reactions.

(Carol K. Sigelman and David R. Shaffer, 1995, p.491)

Healing from grief and loss is a process that can take one, two, or even five years or more, but be encouraged; a new beginning is on the horizon.

Reflection

When we think back on the past events of our lives, we find solace and contentment. Healing begins with grieving the past in order that we can address the present and embrace the future. Be encouraged, don't be afraid to look back, it will bring you full circle.

A Word on Grief

Death, dying and grief come in stages, according to Elisabeth Kubler-Ross, as described in her 1969 book, *On Death and Dying*. It is further noted in Ecclesiastes 3:4 (NKJV), that there is "a time to weep, a time to laugh; a time to mourn, and a time to dance." This is noted as a season.

Society views death and its rituals in many ways. People from different ethnic and racial backgrounds express their grief in practices ranging from restrained emotions to overtly wailing, singing, and dancing.

As I researched information on stages, seasons or models, I was surprised at what I uncovered regarding the process of grief and loss. I found that I was more able to relate to the Parkes-Bowlby model of the grieving process:

Numbness

Yearning

Disorganization

Despair

Reorganization

Let's take a minute and digest these. Maybe you will be able to relate to one or several of them.

Numbness – the first few hours or days after the death of your loved one, the bereaved person is often in a daze, gripped by a sense of unreality and disbelief and almost empty of feelings. Underneath this state of numbness and shock is a sense of being on the verge of bursting, and occasionally painful emotions do break through.   The bad news has not fully registered.

Yearning – as the numbing sense of shock and disbelief diminishes, the bereaved person experiences more and more agony. Grief comes in pangs or waves that typically are most severe from five to fourteen days after death. The grieving person has feelings of panic, bouts of uncontrollable weeping, and physical aches and pains.

According to Parkes and Bowlby, the reaction that most clearly makes grieving different from other kinds of emotional distress is separation anxiety, the distress of being parted from the object of one's attachment. The bereaved person pines and yearns for the loved one and actually searches for the deceased, as if the finality of the loss has not been accepted.

Anger and guilt are also common reactions during these early weeks and months of bereavement. People often become irritable, on the edge, and some-times experience intense rage at the loved one for dying, or at the doctors, at anyone. To make sense of the death, they need to blame someone, even themselves.

Disorganization and Despair. As time passes, pangs of intense grief and yearning become less frequent, though they still occur. As it sinks in that a reunion with the loved one is impossible, depression, despair, and apathy increas-ingly predominate. During the first year after death, and longer, in many cases, bereaved individuals often feel apathetic or even defeated. They may have difficulty managing their lives or taking any interest in activities.

Reorganization – Eventually, bereaved persons begin to pull themselves together again as their pangs of grief and periods of apathy become less frequent. They come to invest less emotional energy in their attachment to the deceased and more in their attachments to the living. If married, they begin to make the transition from being a wife or husband to being a widow or widower, slowly shedding their old identities as individuals. They begin to feel ready for the new activities and possibly for new relation-ships. The decision has been made and it is time to make an attempt to move to the next chapter. The valley is not the place to linger for any period of time.

My Experience

There were times when I thought, if I could just get up, I would be just fine. Of course, there were times when I just decided to stay in bed and cry.

But then, I would get up the next day and begin my chores or work, as if nothing had changed, but everybody knew, I was not the same person. Even though I tried to be the same happy, positive person, it seemed futile. My life was filled with blue days, flashbacks, and shades of gray, in every waking moment. The fog was continuous; heaviness engulfed every fiber of my being. It surrounded me, as if I were in a bubble, no beginning and no end, just as fragile.

The shock of what had occurred caused me to be immobile. My mind and emotions were unable to press forward, you know, "get on with it." *What am I going to do?* I thought. *My life has been put on hold and there seems to be nothing I can do about it.* How could I tell my friends and family that I was in trouble? How could I admit that I felt hopeless and helpless? I was taught that what happened in the family, stayed in the family. This was not so bad; it allowed you to work through family matters by yourself, keeping others, as they say, out of your business. But I realized something. I needed somebody in my business! I just didn't know who.

People had said to me, "Stay strong; don't give in to your feelings." Oh, and there have been those who said, "You know, this too shall pass." *Wow!* I thought, *This too shall pass!? Really? What on earth could that possibly mean?*

There were also those who said, "You have to move on with your life, get over it." Get over it? You must be kidding! How do you get over loving someone, for what seems to be the majority of your adult life? Get over it? How do you get over the love of your life, your best friend, confidant and lover being gone? Get over it! *Well*, I thought…*go to hell! You get over it!!*

It was clear, I was irritable! Not only irritable, but I was angry! Oh, I tried to conceal it, but I knew people could tell that I wasn't the same. So I decided to become isolated; remove myself from friends and family. I felt people were tired of seeing the tears, fed up with hearing about my pain, and impatient with seeing my sadness.

I was officially down; deep in the valley. A place where the hopelessness and helplessness dwelt. It seemed that I would stay in this desolate place forever.

In the valley, there were streams. The streams were the tears I would shed, seamlessly, never-ending and constantly flowing. The hills in the valley were barren, lifeless, with little or no beauty. This was me, no beauty, no life, and the horrible thought that I would never have a productive future.

The Wife of a Vietnam Veteran

I am the wife of a Vietnam veteran, a man who suffered at the hands of an enemy. This suffering followed him from Vietnam to Chicago. His wounds lay dormant for several decades. However, Honey's inner man never got over the pain of war. My Honey's wounds festered, eating at the very core of his humanity, his manhood, and his quest for peace.

He finally did find peace — though, at the end of the day. The day he went home to be with the Lord. Prior to that day, he would have moments of joy, deep on the inside, because of his faith. He loved the old spirituals and at times sang them. They sounded very good.

I would tease him and say, "You better not quit your day job," and we would both laugh. And then he would be still and quiet, and began to talk about his life, as a child, and his life as a soldier. Honey loved family, but he lamented over the loss of his youth.

He would say, "War does that, you know, to a young man. It just takes away the smiles of your youth." He was determined to continue his quest for life, even with all the obstacles in his path.

I have often wondered how the soldiers' wives of today are coping with the conflicted feelings that they encounter. Uncertain about the feelings, moods, hurt, and anger that their husbands are experiencing. I see the soldiers coming home and being welcomed, and remember that when my husband came home, there was no welcome. Back then, soldiers were called "baby killers." Honey would cry when he would hear those piercing words. Yet he felt such gratitude when the soldiers came home from Iraq, because they were treated with dignity. How could anyone mistreat any soldier who leaves his family to go to foreign shores, just to keep our shores free?

I still wonder how these women are coping with the torn limbs of despair and confusion, the far away looks of betrayal, and the uncertainty of their future. I still wonder!

While I am wondering, I pray for them and their husbands. I ask God to protect them while they are away and return them home, safe and whole. I am a counselor, by profession, and I have seen pain and suffering experienced by others. However, I still wonder about the journey of these women.

War is a bittersweet experience for the men and women who fight in them. Torn emotions are absorbed with each breath, and surrounded by inner silence; they search for a moment of peace. My husband spoke highly of the military, even though he suffered physically and emotionally. He often said God kept him and returned him home, and he would always be thankful. To God be the glory!!

CHAPTER FOUR

THE VALLEY
IS NOT AN OPTION

*I*t had been over a year now, and I realized that I could not spend my life reflecting and looking back. I decided to call my friend, Rebecca and talk to her. As I was dialing, I thought, *Oh, I'll hang up, this is a mistake!*

At that very moment, someone answered, "Hello."

"Hello, Rebecca."

"Dot! Oh my goodness, how wonderful to hear your voice! It has been such a long time!"

"Yes, it has Rebecca."

"How've you been?" Her voice was soft and tender.

"I haven't been doing that well, but I am ready to do better."

"I'm here for you, Dot. I always have been."

"I know you have," I said. "I called to see if you were free for coffee. I would love to see you and talk."

"Tell you what, Dot, Jerry is out of town, why don't you come to my house? We'll have a sleepover and we can talk as long as you need."

I thought for a minute and agreed. We both began to laugh and Rebecca said, "This will be just like old times, when we used to travel together."

"You're right. I'll be over later this afternoon. Thank you, Rebecca."

"No, thank you, my friend."

We hung up the phone and I began to weep and pray. "Thank you, Lord, for the courage to reach out to my friend. Continue to give me the courage to come out of the fog. I am ready now, truly ready. Thank you, Lord, thank you."

Rebecca and I had been friends for a long time. Since Honey's death, we had drifted apart because of my valley experience. I missed our friendship and was ready to move forward with my life, rekindling friendships and reconnecting with family. Today was a good day I thought, and I was excited about seeing my friend. I had not felt this way for a long time.

As I began to pack my bag, I decided to call my children to check in with them. I talked with them on a daily basis; however, they had continued to insist that I contact Rebecca. I told them that I was spending the night with Rebecca. Their response was one of excitement and relief.

After pulling up in front of Rebecca's house, I just sat there for what seemed to be an hour. I remembered the last time I was here. Honey and I had attended a party they had given. I recalled us having so much fun; old school dancing,

Scrabble, and karaoke. Honey talked about that party for days. These memories brought laughter to my heart and I began to smile...then, it hit me. I smiled! I hadn't smiled at a memory of him since his death.

"Dot," Rebecca called out, "are you going to stay in the car?"

"Of course not," I shouted back.

"Pull in the driveway, will you?"

"All right."

"Hey girl!"

"Hey yourself."

We hugged and we both began to weep.

"How good it is to see you," I said.

"Glad to see you, too. I have prepared something to eat for us, and of course, I have your coffee."

"That's great, I could use a Latte."

"No problem your coffee shop is now open," replied Rebecca. She had all the coffee trimmings in her kitchen. She had experimented with different kinds of coffees and used me as her taste tester. Rebecca had wanted to open her own coffee shop someday, and her dream was still alive. "Here's your special mixture. "

"This is good, Rebecca, a cup to keep."

"Now, my friend, let's get your bags upstairs and then we will sit on the sun porch and talk."

I slowed my steps in reminiscence as I passed the billiards room. Honey would tease Bob about the sign on the wall; Bob's Billiards Room.

He would say, "Man, you know this is just a fancy pool table, with all the fixins," and they would laugh, and of course, rack 'em up and began to talk 'stuff.' Good memories.

"Now, Dot! Your bags are in your room, let's go sit outside."

"I love this porch. It's very comfortable."

"Please, tell me how you've been."

I answered Rebecca with my head down. "I haven't been doing well. I am sad most of the time, feelings of emptiness and extreme loneliness. I seem to cry all the time and I am tired of it, but I don't know how to move forward." I started to weep again, saying, "Oh, how I miss him."

I continued to talk about my travels in the valley, as I called it.

"How long do you plan to stay in this emotional valley, Dot?"

"It was never my plan to be here, I am just here."

"I think you should talk to someone from church. They have trained professionals."

"I know, but I would rather not, maybe I can see someone from your church? You know, confidentiality and all."

"I know, but I don't think that would be a problem at your church," Rebecca said.

"Of course not, I know I'm being silly, but indulge me this, will you."

"All right. There are people in my church who are trained and licensed as therapists who specialize in grief counseling. I think that is what you need."

"I know I need something. I can't continue in this fog."

"He loved you very much. He would not want your life to be at a standstill. You are still a very vibrant woman with so much to offer your children, grandchildren, family and friends. In addition, maybe you can begin to think about writing that book you always talked about."

The sun was going down now. What a beautiful orange ball, just sitting in the sky, waiting for the time to disappear.

"Dot," Rebecca called out. "I just had an idea."

"What is it?"

"You always wanted to take a cruise around the world. Maybe you should think about doing something like that."

"I don't want to be gone that long, Rebecca."

"What about a month? I think the travel would do you a world of good. You love the ocean; really any body of water is fine with you." We laughed and I agreed.

"I think you are right. This would be wonderful. I will take the time off, can you arrange some time?"

"Tell you what, I'll go with you to… Aruba, for two weeks?"

"Who said Aruba?"

"I thought you did."

"Sure you did." We both laughed.

"I'll call Cheryl, she is a friend who owns a travel agency. She would love to plan this for us. In addition, you can come home for a week, and then continue on to Maine to write."

Dare I!? *Maybe*, I thought. *Just maybe.*

CHAPTER FIVE

HEALING BEGINS

When I returned home, the house was just as I'd left it, dark and cold. Suddenly, I decided to open the curtains, allowing the sun to take some of the darkness away. I began to look out the window and I noticed that the wind was blowing, lifting the leaves from the trees. *Oh my,* I thought, *I haven't noticed the leaves in a long time.*

I sat on the sofa and began to think about the trip. For some reason, I was not excited anymore. I wasn't feeling depressed, just not really wanting to take a cruise, now. I wondered why I allowed Rebecca to talk me into this. This thought caused me to chuckle to myself.

While sitting on the sofa, I decided to read a few scriptures, thinking this would bring me comfort. As I began to read, I was led to scriptures about mourning, grief, and, being a widow. I read until the sun was no longer shining, forcing me to leave the Word for a moment to close the curtains and turn on the lamp. The supremacy of God, through His word was so powerful. I felt a sudden calm-ness and inner contentment. I knew I *had* to get a grip on my life. I was in a state of denial, causing me to withdraw from everything and everyone. This would be detrimental and lead me to a place that was unhealthy and emotionally unsafe.

Maybe I will take this trip. It will be fun and maybe just what I need.

I had to begin the voyage of healing. It would take me places inside myself that I needed to tread upon lightly, even though in the beginning, the treading would be light. Where would I get the strength, to go down this road?

Aruba

The day had arrived and the limo was waiting for me outside. We picked up Rebecca and were on our way to the airport.

"Are you excited yet?"

"Yes, I am. Rebecca, I'm so glad you talked me into taking this cruise. We are finally here. Wow! This ship is absolutely beautiful."

We checked in and began to walk around the huge vessel. Our cabin was great and had a window where I could see the water and look at each port when we docked. I felt serene, at peace, not caring about the next day, just thinking about the here and now. I spent time crying and laughing at some of the good times. I would look out at the ocean and only see an endless flow of waves. With each wave, I thought, *Here is another milestone I must overcome, another obstacles I must confront.*

Healing, well, it was about to take place. The days passed quickly. We had fun visiting different islands and meeting new people. I spent a lot of time in the evening on deck.

I awoke one morning to watch the sunrise. I had never seen anything so powerful. It looked as if the sun was on the edge of the ocean and shone against the backdrop of the sky. God is truly awesome! I thought more and more about writing my manuscript and how that could be very cathartic for me.

*****

The trip was wonderful. However, the plane had landed and I was home. Rebecca and I said our goodbyes. She was headed to Paris to meet her husband. The limousine pulled up in front of my house, and I dreaded going in alone. But to my surprise, my prayers had been answered and I was able to once again live in my house. Oh, it was still difficult, but I was thankful that it was now bearable. I was still in the valley, but now I was willing to begin my journey, one that would take me to a place of discovery.

> *Healing from grief and loss*
> *is a process that can take one,*
> *two or even five years or more,*
> *but be encouraged; a new beginning*
> *is on the horizon.*

Reflection

When we think back on the past events of our lives, we find solace and content- ment.

Healing begins with grieving the past, in order that we can address the present and embrace the future.

Be encouraged, don't be afraid to look back, it will bring you full circle.

PART TWO ~ SEASON ONE
MY JOURNEY THROUGH THE
MAZE OF HEALING

What causes one to wonder if the universe is truly a place for love, death, and continuance? I have asked myself this question for a long time now. It seems that the love part is very easy, or is it? I loved a man once, for what seemed to be most of my life. We loved and our children were born from this love. We grew as a couple, and of course, we grew up as individuals. The love lasted for forty years and abruptly — it was gone. How, you may ask? Well, our love was taken away, in the cold darkness of night. Snatched by the Grim Reaper, as he is called by some, but we know him as Death.

The love of my life was no longer warm and vibrant, but cold and still. Traveling now on a distant shore, where the waves of hope had diminished, and the fire in his eyes was no longer …. he sleeps.

I have asked myself, "What becomes of a broken heart?" My answer is, "It stays broken for a while, until the journey of mourning, grief, and healing have been completed." I invite you to join me as I travel through the highs and lows, ups and downs, ins and outs, of misery, heart-ache, despair, and finally, healing.

~~~~~~~~~~~~~~~

After all the people left and the funeral was over, I found myself alone and frightened. The tears began to flow as if the floodgates had been released from a large reservoir. I cried non-stop until I fell asleep, only to be awakened and begin the cycle of non-stop crying all over again.

This is so cruel, I thought, *to be left behind, in a pit of loneliness. Who would love me?* I thought. *Who would hold me, who would be my best friend and companion?* My mind could only embrace the negative side of loss, no room for hope, no comfort in sight for me.

My husband was a kind and loving man, filled with hopes and dreams for our later years. Some of his dreams would come to fruition, and some would not. But know for sure, we loved, oh my goodness, did we love. One might say that we truly completed each other. Soul mates—you bet we were!

Once the frequency of the tears began to subside, the hollowness began to take over. I couldn't imagine what emptiness felt like, but soon, I came face-to-face with the reality of this feeling. I continued to wonder about the process of grief and its stages. Of course I knew what they were—due to my profession —- but never had experienced the stages and its processes.

I guess I was in the sad or depressed stage. Sadness became my best friend for a while, allowing no one else to be my companion. Sadness and I went to work

together, meetings together, had meals —
when I would eat — together, and oh yes,
we slept together. Sometimes, sadness
and I only got out of bed when it was
seriously necessary, you know, for work
or hygienic reasons. And then, it was a
struggle, because sadness did not want to
let me go.

At times, sadness and I would bring
along a friend, anger. Anger was subtle,
but at times she would raise her ugly
head. She had no patience with people,
family, or friends. Anger would take sadness and overwhelm her, causing sadness
to quietly disappear.

Despair, loneliness, anger, depression,
forgiveness, and acceptance are some of

the characteristics of the grief and loss journey — at least, the ones I encountered.

As we take this journey, I will share what got me through each season.

Weeping, Weeping, Weeping

Sadness, I found, was a state of hollowness. Here you were empty, as if whatever feelings you had were suddenly swallowed up by the dark mystery of pain. And that pain for me was as sharp as a knife, cutting through the toughest piece of meat you could find. Sadness is defined by *Webster's Unabridged Dictionary* as being affected by unhappiness or grief, very sorrowful. Well, this was indicative of the emotion that was a constant for me for a very long time.

There were times when I would smile, yet deep within my heart there was a large hole that needed immediate repair. This was a time that some might say would last only for a few weeks or months, then it would go away forever. Maybe this was true for some; however, the times of sadness and the feelings of emptiness lasted for more than a few weeks. Fortunately, I was able to evoke a pleasant memory of happier times.

How to cope:

When I encountered sadness, there were several things I would do. After the tears and sobbing, I would sit quietly for hours, silent, listless, and numb. At first, I was only able to sit. Sometimes I would sleep.

Meditation & Prayers

As time passed, I began to search the Bible for scriptures that addressed the feeling of sadness. One that ministered to my heart most often can be found in Psalm 30:5, which states in part:

> "Weeping may endure for a night, But joy comes in the morning."

> I looked forward to a time of joy in my heart, knowing that God is a healer of the heart.

Another favorite comes from Isaiah 61:3, and it says:

"To console those who mourn in Zion, To give them beauty for ashes, The oil of joy for mourning, The garment of praise for the spirit of heaviness; That they may be called trees of righteousness, The planting of the Lord, that He may be glorified."

As time passed, I began to meditate and pray, for instance, "Lord, comfort me." Then, the prayers became longer, more intense, and fervent. At this point I began to petition God for guidance and help. This was extremely calming for me and allowed me a chance to commune with God.

Of course, most people hate to exercise, and I think I rank among the worse, probably number two in a scale of 1-10, with ten being the highest. But to my surprise, I began to walk, breathing in the crisp winter air and the warm breezes of summer. This increase of adrenaline caused me to feel better, almost serene at times.

Journaling

Sometimes, I would write my feelings in my journal. I recommend that you began journaling as you travel down this road. The journey is long and complicated. Writing helps you to release those feelings, and later, review this part of your journey with promise. When we talk about the need to express our feelings and emotions, we are sometimes hesitant about sharing with others. Writing is always an alternative.

The Bible was one of the first books that I read that emphasized the importance of writing. I remember learning about The Ten Commandments and watching the movie. How could we possibly forget "Moses," played by Charleston Heston? In the movie and in the Bible, the words, "It Is written," are quoted over and over again. Also, Exodus 31:18 speaks about the "Handwriting of God." Finally, I read in Jeremiah 30:2, that God gave Jeremiah instructions to "write in a book," the things that God told him.

With this revelation, I am compelled to believe that the power of the written word is not only intended for knowledge, but also for healing and restoration. Therefore, journaling could possibly be the key to begin suturing a broken heart.

When I encountered anger, first I had to settle down! Anger would overwhelm me at times, with outbursts of frustration. Snapping and even raising my voice would become a part of my temporary make-up. Usually, this was kept among those with whom I felt safe; however, at times, she would spill over to the un-safety zone. Prayer and meditation would always bring me back into focus.

There were times when my anger would concentrate on what I will refer to as the act of betrayal. My husband left me, of course not on his own, but the emotions would come in flurries that seemed to dominate the moment. I would blame him for leaving me alone to face a world that is cruel, unforgiving, and unjust to women. I felt unprotected and left to fend for myself. Oh anger, she was crafty and would cause me to become isolated and withdraw from those who loved me.

Anger is an emotion that can range from feelings of abandonment to episodes of rage or fury. My sadness lingered for such a long time that I never considered it as being anger. As time passed, my emotions began to shift. I felt alone and betrayed. I thought, *How could he leave me like this? Who will be there for me, who will help me when I am confronted with the trials of this life? Who will be my best friend, my confidant, who would I share my funny stories with and the troubles of my day? Who could I talk to about the kids, their problems, and their joys? Who would be there with me to share the smiles and laughter of the grandchildren?*

"Oh God!" I screamed on many occasions. "Why would Honey leave me now, when our lives were so good and retirement plans were just a couple of years away? Why?" I thought. "Why?" My anger intensified to a point of throwing glasses toward the floor. Loud sounds engulfed the room. Finally, I began to cry, and as I sat on the floor, I found relief.

After a few days, going back and forth through this maze of anger and sadness, I once again retreated to my safe place: the Word of God. I would recall a scripture and began to read it, sometimes aloud, just to hear the power of the Word.

First, I had to strip away anger by allowing the Word of God to penetrate my heart. James 1:19-20 states:

> "So then, my beloved breth-ren, let every man be swift to hear, slow to speak and slow to wrath; for the wrath of man does not produce the righ-teousness of God."

My anger was soothed by the love I had for others and the love I still had for God. **Remember, anger and hate are always defeated by love.**

Season one lasted for a long time, mostly the sadness. But as the days, weeks, months, and years passed, so did the intensity of the pain of this season. Praise God for victory!

SEASON TWO
DISTRACTIONS, DISTRACTIONS, DISTRACTIONS

*T*his time was one of desperation and despair. Not knowing what, when or how one's life could spin could be overwhelming. Uncertainty, to say the least, causes anxiety, yet fear can creep in and stay a while. This was an especially difficult time for me. My husband and I had shared everything. Sometimes we could finish each other's thoughts, and laugh about it. But now, my life had been turned upside down, with a future that seemed as dark as the depths of the ocean and as frightening as a bird whose wing was broken.

The first area of desperation was in the region of money matters. How to make sure that the budget was current or should I say, revising it to reflect a more objective picture. I have heard some women say that they were afraid to confront issues of money because they were not comfortable. Their husbands had handled everything and they just didn't know where to begin. Well, be encouraged, begin at the beginning.

Seek advice from a financial expert, for example, your banker, tax accountant, or financial advisor. They are professionals and will not be biased, but objective. I worked with all three and was able to get on an effective and efficient track very quickly, and to my surprise, the stressors in this area were manageable.

I am reminded of the scriptures. One in particular:

> "We are hard pressed on every side, yet not crushed; we are perplexed, but not in despair." 2 Corinthians 4:8.

Another area of desperation for me was the dilemma of where I would live. Oh, I was not homeless, just the opposite. I had a very lovely home, with rooms that were left empty. My challenge was staying in the house alone. I could still smell his aftershave, sometimes early in the morning. I would wake up reaching for him, and then realize that his side of the bed was empty. I would sit at the kitchen table, and look across, and it too was empty. There were overwhelming urges at times to run away from home. Sometimes, I did. I would spend weekends with my girlfriends or with my sons. This emotion was also accompanied by fear. I was not accustomed to being home alone, and this was strange and scary for me. I heard noises that I'd never heard before. Coming home nights, I was afraid to get out of the car. I was used to my husband waiting for me on our porch. Customarily, I would call him to let him know I was turning onto our block, and he would always, I mean always, be there waiting for me. The thought that he would never be waiting for me again was, at times, more than I could bear. Comfort me, Lord Jesus. Comfort me! This was the quick prayer I would repeat on a consistent basis. God was faithful and always gave me comfort and relief.

There were times when I felt a sense of hopelessness and gloom. Despair can cause you to manifest these feelings, even though you try hard to hold on to hope.

The Bible teaches us to hold on to God, and not fear.

> "Wait on the Lord, be of good courage, and He shall strengthen your heart: Wait, I say, on the Lord." Psalm 27:14

"He gives power to the weak,
And to those who have no
might He increases strength.
Even the youths shall faint
and be weary, And the young
men shall utterly fall, But
those who wait on the Lord
Shall renew their strength;
They shall mount up with
wings like eagles, They shall
run and not be weary, They
shall walk and not faint."
Isaiah 40:29-31

Waiting was all I could do. Nothing else
seemed to help. The voyage of waiting
was long and tumultuous, and at times
presented with feelings of agitation. As

humans, we have such difficulty waiting and being patient with our circumstances. However, we must remember what the Bible says:

> "Hope deferred makes the heart sick, But when the desire comes, it is a tree of life." Proverbs 13:12.

The time of despair was short-lived, even though it seemed endless. The darkness of gloom was ever-present, until the light of hope was revealed.

Our relationship experienced the forty-year mark, which clearly reflected God's blessings upon our marriage. The number forty has a significant meaning according to the theology of numerology.

"It is the product of five and eight, and points to the action of grace (five), leading to and ending in revival and renewal (eight). A forty something time period, whether days, month, or years is always a period of testing, trial, probation or chastisement (but not judgment) and ends with a period of restoration, revival or renewal."

(Source: http://belovedheart.wordpress.)

The testing period was a time of great suffering for us during Honey's illness; however, my inner self was being revived, as if being resuscitated after a long absence. It was almost as if I had been asleep, walking and talking but not really present in the here and now. The renewal was near on the horizon, waiting the dawning of a fresh new day.

This season closed with a feeling of refreshing and anticipation. *Praise God for Victory!*

SEASON THREE
ISOLATION, DESOLATION, LOST

This season seemed to be never-ending. Grief can cause feelings that you never imagined you would experience. I never felt that I would withdraw from friends and family. However, to my surprise, I did. It seemed to occur slowly, calculatedly, with precise purpose and intent. To my chagrin, I was noticeably stunned when confronted about this apparent behavior. I must admit that I didn't feel the need to object to the observations of my friends; however, I didn't feel the need to make changes. I didn't have the patience for the looks of pity and self- righteousness exhibited by some well-meaning associates.

I felt lost and without purpose. How could I possibly possess feelings of belonging and oneness when it didn't exist anymore? Isolation felt safe, not having to look into the eyes of family and dear friends, knowing their thoughts were being reflected through the mirrors of their eyes. I felt compelled to pen these thoughts that I now share with you.

Loneliness

Oh how deep the crevices of an

exposed heart,

Each vessel exposing a torn part.

The beat which pumped love and cheer,

Is only heard with the tone of tears.

Loneliness, why do you linger here?

Go from me so I do not fear.

My heart is wounded.

Why do you stay?

For now, go from me and come back

another day!

Again, my thoughts began to shift and I remembered a place I had visited once while on vacation. It was an environment closely mirroring a desert; hot, dry, and picturesque. This seemed to mimic this time and this season. I, like the desert, felt hot, as if a fire deep in the wells of my inner self was being unveiled. I no longer felt the moisture of love and devotion, but dryness and betrayal. These feelings were insurmountable and engulfed the very fiber of my essence. I walked around every day with a façade, on the surface very together, even beautiful at times, like a picture in a painting, far away, yet close enough to touch. The desert of life contains many beautiful surroundings, just like the desert in Aruba, Arizona; you know: Cacti, rocks, sand, creeping things.

The emotions that flourish during this season of dryness are manifested in aloofness, hardness, moving away from any attempt to attach. Standing in the shadow, looking for shade, however, the sun of life yields no relief. *Move quickly*, I thought, *this is not a season or place you want to linger for any length of time.* Praise God, the desert time has moved far from me!

As the journey continued, the feelings of loss, with no hope of being found, were slowly commencing to subside. My purpose was unfolding, as if watching my life, my dreams, and sense of wonderment moved in slow motion. I would move with it at a pace that God saw fit for me.

SEASON FOUR
THE MAZE

*H*ave you ever wondered how labyrinths are made? How landscapers create such beautiful pieces of art with flowers and evergreens? One of my favorite curiosities is the maze. This design creates a path with a beginning and end that seems never to come into view. During this season, my life was upside down and confusing. It appeared that with each turn, I was faced with obstacles and arrows facing the wrong way. I thought that I would be able to live in the house and face the realization that he was gone—forever. Well, I began to face this dilemma head on, or so I thought. The house became a chain, with never-ending links. I felt as if each door held a room of gloom and doom. I was hesitant to enter rooms with memories of a time of joy and happiness, so I only entered them when it was absolutely necessary. First, it was one room, then another and then another. *Well*, I thought. *Where can I find comfort and solace?* It seemed that the maze was getting longer and never-ending.

The house was not the only area of confusion. I found it painful to attend functions, even church, where his presence was familiar. My work was comforting, but the joy and sense of fulfillment had vanished. The maze was, once again, never-ending.

Finally, I would revert back to a familiar place where peace reigned. This place was the Word of God, found in the Holy Bible. Prayer, reading, and communing with God would always give me relief during the storms in my life.

I made a decision during this season. I decided to change my environment. This was a very difficult decision; however, it was one I had to make. I waited three years before coming to grips with the finality of the situation. Once this happened, then I knew what I needed to do to prepare myself for the journey of restoration and healing.

I resigned from my job and sold my house. I said, *See you later,* to my friends and family and moved to another state. Change, they say, is constant. I have experienced a great deal of change over the years. But finally, I could see clearly now and the end of the maze was in clear sight!

SEASON FIVE

ACQUIESCENCE ~ ACCEPTING THE THINGS I CANNOT CHANGE

"Love is a many-splendored thing," according to a song I heard a long time ago, and comes interestingly, at this time in my life. As I continue on this journey, I realize that this is a true statement. For me, love is a tender moment after a long summer rain, the dew on freshly cut grass, soft and refreshing. It is a stare from across the room, with no need for words, a touch that lingers for days at a time. Love is a smile during life's stormy times. Love is the heart beating in sync with someone else's heart. Love is hope after pain.

I had experienced a love that lasted through the annals of time, the depth of which overshadowed the complexity of the sea. Love, YES! Much Love.

As powerful and intense as this love was, there is NOTHING! that compares to the love that God has for me. The Bible says:

> "Greater love has no one than this, than to lay down one's life for his friends." John 15:13.

It is because Jesus loves me so, that I am able to face tomorrow. That He continues to keep me safe and shields me with His hedge of protection is also confirmation of His love for me. How blessed I am, that I serve a God of love and forgiveness. Thank You, Lord!

My faith has allowed me to forgive the thoughts of betrayal and abandonment. The anger and resentment that clouded my heart and mind have been put to rest. Acceptance, for me, is learning to live one day at a time, just as we are instructed by God.

Believing that God will provide for me, in the absence of my husband, and sustain me as His child, is how I became victorious!

Finally, I trusted that He would make the crooked paths straight, and the rocky roads smooth in every area of my life.

No, I cannot change the fact that the love of my life is absent from me, but I believe that he is present with the Lord, and this is exactly where I am striving, one day at a time, to be. To God be the glory, for the things He has done!

FROM WIFE TO WIDOW

During this journey, I found myself in the midst of chaos, bewilderment, confusion, and fear of the unknown. I realized I had to accept the position of being a widow, which meant I was now single, rather than a wife, which also meant that I had all the rights and dispensations of remarrying; very scary, to say the least. I had to confront a myriad of adjustments, just to be able to function in society. Widows are emotionally, physically, financially, and socially preyed upon, and in some cases ostracized.

When you are married, you function as a couple. Your social interests include friends, family, colleagues, and acquaintances who view you as a part of a set, which includes you and your spouse. Consequently, you are invited to attend functions or gatherings where you are expected to be accompanied by your spouse. Such was the case with me. It became very difficult to attend dinners or an array of social activities alone. I often felt like the third wheel or the odd man out. I'm sure you know the feeling. It became arduous attending church services. At times, I could feel the stares of sympathy or pity from well-meaning parishioners. My solution, I thought, would be to become isolated or attend as few activities as possible, with the exception of those where my attendance would be expected; for example, family gatherings.

The emotional adjustments impacted my physical health. My nerves were frayed, and when periods of sadness and depression would mount I would retreat to a place of comfort. Unfortunately, once again, it would be my bed or total isolation from the outside world.

My health began to deteriorate, with episodes of weight gain and weight loss, up and down like a yo-yo. My body would exhibit physical symptoms of painful headaches, back and knee pain, and elevated blood pressure. *What is going on?* I thought.

Depression can manifest itself with physical as well as emotional pain. This was an adjustment that I knew had to be addressed. Grief counseling provided me the support and reinforcement I needed at the time. *So many adjustments to make with so little time,* I would recall thinking, at times with a smile.

How do I handle the money matters? This would be the ultimate question, or so I thought. Since handling financial matters was a thought out process, sometimes a hassling situation, I was accustomed to making these decisions in conjunction with my husband. I was aware of the banking procedures, understanding bank statements and associated financial strategies. However, once I began to embark on this mind-boggling task alone, it became extremely overwhelming, especially major financial decisions, such as selling or buying a house, retirement planning, and investments such as revising an annuity. These were epic adjustments for me, moving from wife to widow. Simply put, drowning on dry land. One of the major things that I discovered was the absolute necessity of implementing a process of self-care.

We are so busy taking care of our husbands, children, grandchildren, parents, and others that we forget that we need to take care of ourselves. For so long, we have been socialized to be caretakers. One must wonder: Who takes care of us? Hmm! Well, I pondered the question and decided, through it all, at the end of the day, it's Jesus and me.

I started at the beginning and developed a regimen of what I called "health-care in action." I made appointments with my doctors and submitted myself to all the required tests and observations. Praise God, my physical health was good. In an effort to talk through so much of the emotional baggage, I received a litany of spiritual and emotional counseling that allowed me to move forward and broach the gray areas. Praise God for the victory!

I began a sustained prayer life, a health exercise and eating program, including relaxation and proper breathing techniques. I increased my journaling, writing down my feelings. It seemed that the more I practiced honesty on those pages, the more I began to feel peace on the inside.

I found that prayer and meditation were a gift that I had left on the table, picking it up only when needed. Instead, I am involved now on a daily basis, enjoying the true power and beauty of God's earth. I spend hours meditating, listening and watching the birds, noticing the wind as it softly kisses the trees, inspired by the colors of the flowers and moved, some-times to tears, by the sweet smell of lilac. What a wonderful God we serve.

Taking care of yourself is not an act of selfishness, but one of love. When we take care of ourselves, we can love each other more, respect each other without resentments, and truly care for one another.

Tips For Growth

As you go through your individual struggles with grief, develop a course of action that is tailor made for you. Begin at the beginning, leaving nothing to chance.

1. If you are hurting emotionally, seek out a friend, pastor or counselor for help or advice. Staying in a depressed state can lead to physical decline and or suicidal ideation or thoughts. You could also experience the inability to function with routine activities such as working, hygiene, eating, and sleeping.

2. Get up and move by becoming involved in a daily routine. Having a job is very good because it provides you with an outlet and additional incentive to leave the house. If you are not working, volunteer at your church or at a school. There are many shelters that could use your help. Remember, the focus is to get up and move. Be a part of something that is stimulating. Focus your attention on others rather than being consumed by your own problem of circumstance.

3. Journaling. "Don't bite it, write it," refers to the ability to write down one's feelings versus acting them out in negative ways. We have so many feelings

bottled up inside of us, wanting and needing to escape. This is a mechanism whereby you can release your flood of emotions in the privacy of your journal. What you write is between you and that book of thoughts. Go for it! You will be surprised at the healing power of your words and thoughts. In years to come, as you read back through your journal, you will be able to see the growth.

4. There are so many women whose husbands took care of all financial matters. Confusion and being distraught is putting it mildly, when confronted with this deluge of financial chaos.

Learn how to balance a checkbook and have your banker explain your financial statements to you. Work with a member of a financial institution or a financial advisor to help you manage and be more informed about the state of your financial affairs. Family members will offer to assist you. However, you might want to consider exactly how much information you want them to know. "Food for Thought."

5. Make an appointment with your physician to make sure you are informed about the state of your health. Remember, you have gone through a traumatic life-changing experience, which can impact you not only

emotionally, but physically. Being aware of your health status will give you peace of mind in this area.

6. No man is an island, someone once said. Neither are you. Reacquaint yourself with family and friends who you haven't talked with in a while, and catch up on the latest news. They will be glad to hear from you. Make a lunch date with a former colleague or close friend. Commence feeling the warmth of inclusion in different relationships. Spend time, if possible, with your children, grandchildren, parents, and siblings. This will give you joy and inner strength.

Remember, adjusting and read-justing to the difficult seasons that life throws our way is merely a part of who we are as human beings. Learning to finally accept the changes that life puts us through is a sign of growth and grat-itude. Once this occurs, we are ready to turn the page and move on to the next chapter in our lives.

PART THREE
THE RENAISSANCE ~ RENEWAL

"For I know the plans I have for you, declares the Lord, plans for welfare and not for evil, To give you a future and a hope."

Jeremiah 29:11 (ESV)

To Honey:

"Beloved, how I miss the times we spent together. Your smile, your laughter, your gentleness, and your courage. I miss 'us.' The 'you and me.' But I have arrived at a fork in the road of life. I must now make a decision. Do I continue in the maze of confusion,

loneliness and despair?   Or do I trust God and launch into the deep, allowing Him to continue the process of healing?"

Like the bird with a broken wing, my heart was broken, revealing a gaping wound that could only be healed by the Master Healer. I was taking the high road where healing, renewal, and restoration were truly the order of the day.

Then, one night, at midnight, I suddenly awoke from a light sleep. I stood and looked out the window up at the sky for what seemed like hours. The sky was very black, no stars twinkling, clear and exact. I began to pray. *Lord, I need you. Please…oh God, I'm in so much…pain.* I prayed repeatedly. I prayed until I could no longer hear my voice. Then moaning took over and my body bent itself into a prostrate position on the floor.

The next thing I knew, I was awakened by the chirping sound of birds and sunlight shining brightly through my window. I had fallen asleep on the floor. However, I felt well rested.

Months passed and without notice. The process of healing had begun. God had applied the sutures to my gaping wound. He sutured in the area of motivation. I began to fellowship with friends, family, and my church family. Then He applied the sutures of hope, for I had begun to feel hopeless and helpless.

For the Bible says:

> "God is our refuge and
> strength, A very present help
> in trouble." Psalm 46:1 (NKJV)

During the time I was in trouble, He rescued me. The healing continued. He then began to suture the areas of my heart that were being filtered through my mind. I was confused as to why I was left alone...without my Honey. Yes, I understood, on the surface of life, but my heart was having a problem. God closed the wound of confusion and despair.

The Bible says:

> "Create in me a clean heart,
> O God, And renew a stead-
> fast spirit within me." Psalm
> 51:10 (NKJV)

There were times when the depression and anger would engulf me. God seemed to take His time in this area. He worked with me and through me for the closing of this wound. The emotion of anger and depression was manifested in my mind. He needed to "change my mind, renew my thoughts, and make my heart pure so that my mind would be clean."

The Bible says:

> "Do not be conformed to this world, but be transformed by the renewal of your mind, that by testing you may discern what is the will of God, what is good and acceptable and perfect." Romans 12:2 (ESV)

Even though I have read the Word and I am able to comprehend the scriptures, it was not until I had this personal experience with grief that my relationship with God elevated to another dimension. I know that God is Jehovah-Rapha, my healer, and the One who makes bitter experiences sweet, because He healed me.

I know that He will give you back the things that have been taken from you. He gave me back my mind and confidence. He helped my weak faith by showing me that it was He, Jehovah-Shalom, the God of peace, who gave me peace. He, Jehovah-Jireh, is the One who sees my needs and provides for them. It is He, Jehovah-Shammah, who will never leave or forsake me. He will always be there for me. Hallelujah!

At times it seemed that I would be "down in the valley" for the rest of my life. The valley is a gloomy place that is separated by streams and is filled with fear and depression. It is a dangerous place to be because you can get lost, and never found. In the valley. You are alone.

There is no human touch. You are not surrounded by others, and you do not desire their touch. In the valley, your tears will fill up the stream that flows through it.

From time to time, there is a season in which we must linger in the valley. Sometimes the stay will be short, but sometimes the stay will seem like a lifetime. This valley does not contain green fields of foliage. The honeysuckles will not share their fragrance. The terrain is not suitable for the lilies and the clouds are always gray and heavy, waiting to release torrential rains that are inevitable. No, the valley is not a welcoming place to dwell, but you can and you will leave this place.

The process of healing frequently lingers for days, months, and years. For me, it continues today. Where there was profound sadness, God has replaced it with joy. A joy deep on the inside, permeating through crevices of my heart, and flows to the tiniest vessel in my brain. This is the joy of victory and the joy that sustains you in the time of trouble. This is the joy of victory!

The valley is a place where I found myself wandering in search of something, but I am not sure of what yet. I have found that place. It is called the place of a new beginning. My life has evolved into one that is filled with hope and joy! In fact, I find myself laughing all the time. Sometimes, laughing until my cheeks hurt. Once upon a time, laughter had gone far away from me, but it has returned.

I have truly left my life with my husband behind, putting it in a safe place in my memory. I am treading on the sea of unknown adventures, and it feels wonderful. I recently had this epiphany about second chances. I am starting over, and it seems very new and strange…foreign. Like a young woman who gets her first job or has begun her first day at college. She's excited, yet a little nervous about what lies ahead.

The season of renewal and new birth is here, today, and starts right now. God has given me a second chance to live in the present moments of time. I am no longer in a desert of despair, but a garden of hope, yes, and anticipation! The gray clouds of life have been lifted, only remnants of sadness and despair remain. I envision a time of exploration, wonderment and meaningful friendship. I remember a song that continues to minister to me. The words begin with a revelation, "There is power in the name of Jesus, to break every chain, break every chain, to break every chain. Break Every Chain, by Tasha Cobbs. God is breaking the chains of hopelessness and bondage and releasing the freedom of praise and worship in my life. I am thankful for His consistent blessings!

As I embark upon this rebirth period, I visualize God calling into focus my true purpose, according to His will. I have discerned that God allows us to traverse from one period in time to another, one season to another, to prune us for His purpose. I have no trepidations about the journey upon which I am about to tread.

"The Bible says:

> "Behold, I will do a new thing; now it shall spring forth; shall you not know it? I will even make a way in the wilderness, and rivers in the desert." Isaiah 43:19

But joy

Comes

In the morning light…………

About the Author

$\mathcal{D}$r. Dorothy J. Thomas, Master of Science, Counseling, Doctor of Religious Philosophy, Counseling, Certified Alcohol and Drug Abuse Counselor, Gender Competency Endorsement; is a heartfelt advocate of Behavioral Health and Addiction Pathology. She was the former Director of Addiction Services at a community based hospital, located in Chicago, Illinois. Dr. Thomas has worked in the field of addiction for over twenty years as both a clinician and administrator. In addition to her clinical and administrative skills, she is currently an adjunct instructor at Southwest Tennessee Community College, author, "On The Outside Looking In-Unveiling The Mask". She is a former Radio Personality, columnist ,"N" Recovery, for Girl Friends Health Guide For Everyday Women, is a Consultant, Lecturer and Motivational Speaker . She is a widow , mother and grandmother. She states:

"It is my belief and faith that allows me to continue to venture down the roads less traveled. This is who I am, and this is what I live by."